Wonders of Learning

DISCOVER
SPACE

Find, Stick and Learn

Hours of fun-filled activities about space
for children to read and explore!

Sticker Book

The Night Sky

Did you know that, when you look up into the night sky, you are actually looking out into space? On a clear night you will be able to see the Moon, stars, and even other planets!

Our Solar System is made up of all these bodies, as well as comets, asteroids, minor planets, dust, and gas.

Can you find stickers of all these things and place around the puzzle below?

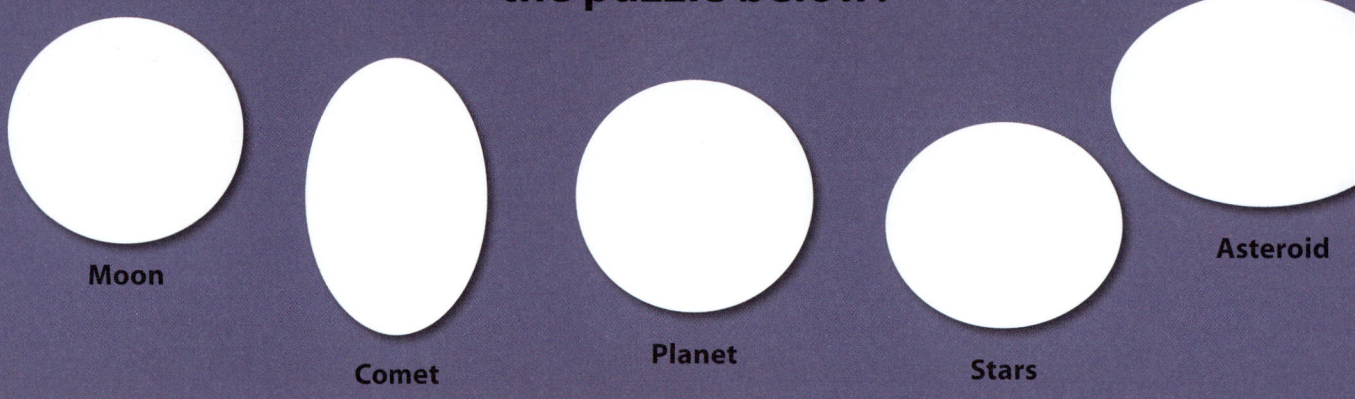

Moon

Comet

Planet

Stars

Asteroid

The Moon

The Moon orbits the Earth at a slight angle, spinning all the time. This means that we can only ever see one half of the Moon's surface from Earth; the other half is known as the "dark side of the Moon"!

As the Moon travels around the Earth, the Sun illuminates different areas of its surface. The lit-up areas change nightly, which is why the Moon looks different at different times.

Look for the stickers of the different phases of the moon and place them here:

Stars

All the stars you can see in the night sky are actually enormous balls of burning gases, like our Sun; they just look tiny because they are so far away.

If you look carefully at the stars on a clear night, you might be able to spot patterns amongst them. These patterns are called constellations. Each constellation is named after the pattern it forms.

See if you can find stickers of some constellations and place them here. Do you think they look like the things they are named after?

Scorpius
is thought to look like a scorpion.

Taurus
looks like the horns of a bull.

Pisces
is named after the Latin word for "fish".

Leo
is named after the Latin word for "lion".

Phases of the Moon

Full Moon

Gibbous Moon

Half Moon

Crescent Moon

New Moon

Galaxies

Stars and their constellations exist in groups called galaxies.

The galaxy that contains our solar system is called the Milky Way.

The Milky Way is a spiral galaxy that contains billions and billions of stars, including our Sun.

The closest galaxy to our Milky Way, the Andromeda Galaxy, is spiral shaped, too, but there are lots of differently shaped galaxies in the Universe: some are egg-shaped, or elliptical, while others form odd, lumpy shapes – these are known as "Irregular Galaxies".

Can you find stickers of the different types of galaxy and place them here?

Spiral Galaxy   **Egg-shaped Galaxy**   **Irregular Galaxy**

Did you know...?

• The first person to journey into outer space was a Russian called Yuri Gagarin; his rocket, Vostok, completed an orbit of the Earth on 12th April 1961.

• Eight years later, on 20th July 1969, an American astronaut called Neil Armstrong became the first man to walk on the Moon.

Wordsearch

How many of the words from the list can you find?

S	P	F	P	A	X	C	F	T	T	J	Y	A	H	Q
U	K	P	F	Z	E	D	Y	N	V	V	L	E	A	S
I	Y	T	G	O	L	X	E	I	H	R	H	Q	M	V
P	R	L	L	Y	A	C	D	C	S	P	Q	S	K	Y
R	Y	L	U	L	S	Y	S	U	O	B	B	I	G	J
O	S	U	A	E	U	R	D	B	A	G	W	G	B	N
C	I	G	R	D	A	H	T	W	S	R	H	K	R	S
S	Q	C	N	T	K	N	X	M	T	B	E	T	K	I
Y	U	P	S	D	P	O	Y	E	E	S	Y	A	G	D
E	N	V	L	K	G	O	K	J	R	E	J	U	F	Z
K	Y	C	O	A	I	M	I	M	O	C	T	R	L	U
E	O	E	A	E	N	L	A	C	I	S	M	U	M	Q
T	X	Z	P	M	V	E	V	M	D	I	Q	S	C	G
A	U	P	Z	S	T	X	T	J	O	P	C	V	V	N
D	R	Y	A	F	T	E	M	O	C	R	Z	L	F	U

GALAXY
STARS
CRESCENT
GIBBOUS
ASTEROID
COMET
MOON
PLANET
TAURUS
PISCES
SCORPIUS

Did You Know?

• On a clear night you will be able to see the Andromeda Galaxy as a smudge in the sky!

• Stars don't only come out at night; they are there all the time, but you can't always see them, because the light from the Sun is so much brighter!

Our Solar System

There are eight planets in our Solar System, as well as a dwarf planet called Pluto.

All orbit the sun, and are held in place by the Sun's gravity, which stops them spinning away into space!

Try jumping up in the air; the reason you come back down again is because the Earth's gravity is acting upon you – without it you would float up into the sky! The Sun's gravity keeps the Earth in place in exactly the same way.

Mercury!

The planet closest to the Sun is also the smallest planet in our solar system, and the fastest moving. It is named after the flying messenger of the Roman Gods, Mercury.

Mercury is very hot and dry during the day, and very cold at night. There is no air or water on the surface, so no living things would be able to survive there.

MERCUR
DISTANCE FROM S
0.39 AU
(58,000,000 km)
LENGTH OF DA
175.9 EARTH days
LENGTH OF YEA
88 EARTH DAYS
TYPE:
TERRESTRIA
0 RINGS 0 MOONS
O Na

Venus

Venus is the closest planet to Earth, and is named after the Roman Goddess of love and beauty. It spins in the opposite direction to most of the other planets, and is covered by an atmosphere of swirling gases.

Venus and Earth are often referred to as sister planets because they are very similar in size!

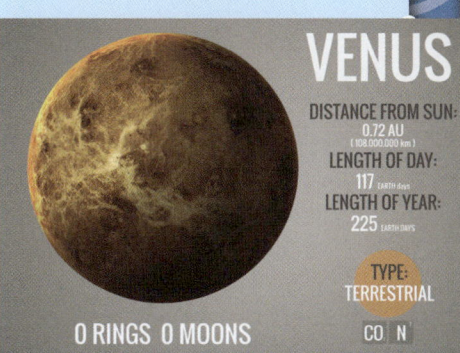

VENUS

DISTANCE FROM SUN:
0.72 AU
(108,000,000 km)
LENGTH OF DAY:
117 EARTH days
LENGTH OF YEAR:
225 EARTH DAYS

TYPE:
TERRESTRIAL

CO N

0 RINGS 0 MOONS

Did you know...?

- The moon is 50 times smaller than the Earth!

- It is covered in boulders, dust, and craters, which were made when rocks from space crashed into the Moon's surface.

- Our sea tides are caused by the pull of the moon on the Earth!

- Occasionally the Sun, the Earth, and the Moon all line up, causing an eclipse.

Earth

The Earth orbits the Sun once every 365 days, which is why there are 365 days in a year. Even though you can't feel it, the Earth is moving around the Sun all the time, travelling at a speed of 66,630 miles an hour!

The Earth spins as it turns, which is why we have day and night: when a country is facing the Sun it is daytime; when it is facing away it becomes dark, and is night.

The tilt of the Earth gives us our seasons: the coldest time of year for a country is when it is tilted farthest away from the Sun.

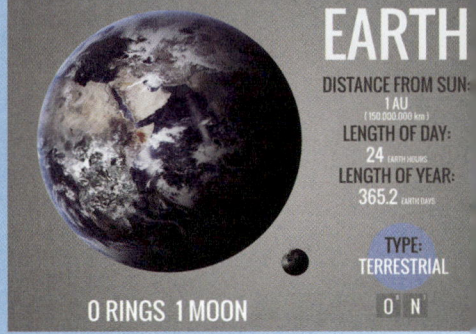

EARTH

DISTANCE FROM SUN:
1 AU
(150,000,000 km)
LENGTH OF DAY:
24 EARTH HOURS
LENGTH OF YEAR:
365.2 EARTH DAYS

TYPE:
TERRESTRIAL

O N

0 RINGS 1 MOON

Mars

Mars is named after the Roman God of War, and is often called the "Red Planet" because of its colour.

The seasons on Mars are extreme, with very hot summers and freezing cold winters. Dust storms are common and can last for months, covering the whole planet, and helping to give it its red colour.

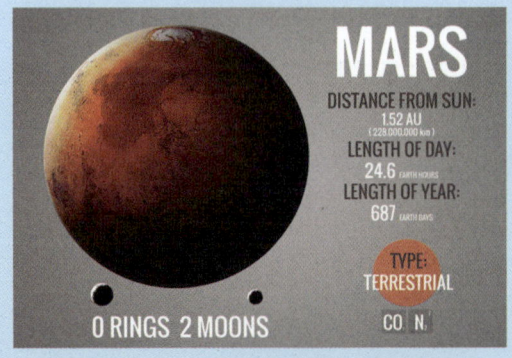

MARS

DISTANCE FROM SUN:
1.52 AU
(228,000,000 km)
LENGTH OF DAY:
24.6 EARTH HOURS
LENGTH OF YEAR:
687 EARTH DAYS

TYPE:
TERRESTRIAL

CO N

0 RINGS 2 MOONS

Wordsearch

How many of the words from the list can you find?

Y	A	Q	D	Q	K	M	A	D	F	F	Q	J	D	B
M	E	T	S	Y	S	R	A	L	O	S	O	C	I	D
R	V	E	N	U	S	C	G	A	V	Q	X	P	Y	M
A	Y	C	X	R	M	M	P	B	X	R	J	B	D	H
I	P	Q	C	I	U	W	I	U	E	Q	P	Z	K	F
G	S	R	G	S	M	T	N	Y	R	U	C	R	E	M
J	E	R	Q	T	U	C	A	E	J	A	Y	T	M	X
Q	H	E	I	E	T	G	Y	S	P	J	N	D	A	N
E	C	T	O	N	C	H	U	P	H	T	P	U	R	F
A	D	I	H	A	T	J	P	C	V	L	U	A	S	D
R	J	P	E	L	B	M	W	H	U	R	U	N	Q	R
T	P	U	U	P	V	O	L	T	O	V	B	O	E	C
H	H	J	L	D	W	G	O	E	X	S	R	B	F	Y
R	D	X	G	J	Q	D	N	Y	P	W	L	G	J	Q
E	V	S	M	H	B	T	K	Q	W	P	V	D	Y	J

VENUS   SATURN

MARS   URANUS

JUPITER   NEPTUNE

PLUTO   SOLARSYSTEM

MERCURY   PLANETS

EARTH

The Gas Giants

Jupiter

Jupiter is the largest planet in our Solar System and is named after the Roman King of the Gods. It is two and a half times bigger than all of the other planets put together!

Because it is so large, Jupiter's gravity is very strong, and has often pulled passing objects into its orbit. Many of these have become Jupiter's moons, and orbit the planet in the same way as our moon travels around the Earth.

Jupiter has at least 63 moons; the largest, Ganymede, is bigger than the planet Mercury!

Did you know...?

- There is a hurricane on Jupiter that has raged for at least 350 years! The storm so big that three planet Earths could fit inside it, and is known as the Great Red Spot.

JUPITER

DISTANCE FROM SUN:
5.2 AU
(778,000,000 km)
LENGTH OF DAY:
9.9 EARTH HOURS
LENGTH OF YEAR:
11.8 EARTH YEARS

TYPE:
GAS GIANT

3 RINGS 67 MOONS   H He

WARNING

Saturn

Saturn is named after the Roman God of agriculture, and, like Jupiter, Uranus, and Neptune, is surrounded by rings made up of rocks, dust, and ice.

As well as it's rings, Saturn has at least 150 moons and moonlets. It is the most distant planet that can be seen with the naked eye.

Did you know...?

• Saturn is so light that if you could find a bathtub big enough to put it in, the whole planet would float!

SATURN

DISTANCE FROM SUN:
9.5 AU
(1,400,000,000 km)
LENGTH OF DAY:
10.5 EARTH HOURS
LENGTH OF YEAR:
29.4 EARTH YEARS

TYPE:
GAS GIANT

H   He

7 RINGS 62 MOONS

Uranus

Uranus is invisible to the naked eye, and was the first planet to be discovered using a telescope.

Uranus is surrounded by rings, and has 27 known moons, which are all named after characters in English literature!

Did you know...?

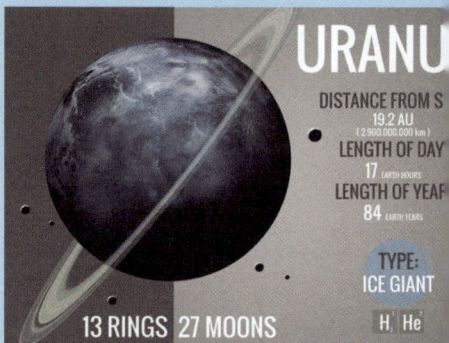

URANU

DISTANCE FROM S
19.2 AU
(2,900,000,000 km)
LENGTH OF DAY
17 EARTH HOURS
LENGTH OF YEAR
84 EARTH YEARS

TYPE:
ICE GIANT

H₂ He

13 RINGS 27 MOONS

• Night can last for forty years on the parts of Uranus facing away from the Sun!

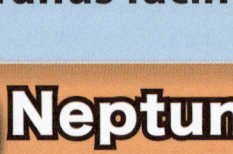

Neptune

Neptune is named after the Roman God of the Sea, and, like the other Gas Giants, is surrounded by rings and moons. One of its moons, Triton, is thought to be the coldest world in the entire Solar System!

Did you know...?

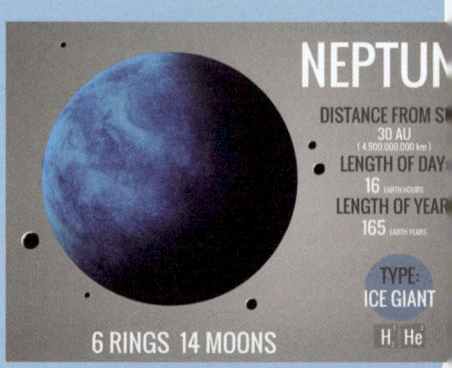

NEPTUN

DISTANCE FROM S
30 AU
(4,500,000,000 km)
LENGTH OF DAY
16 EARTH HOURS
LENGTH OF YEAR
165 EARTH YEARS

TYPE:
ICE GIANT

H₂ He

6 RINGS 14 MOONS

• Violent storms are common on Neptune. The Great Dark Spot was one of the largest ever recorded, and lasted for about five years!

Can you match each of these facts with the planet they belong to? See if you can find stickers of each planet to put in the column on the right:

Planet closest to the Sun

Spins in the opposite direction to all the other planets

Our home planet

The Red Planet

The largest of all the planets

This planet has over 150 moons

Night can last for 40 years on this planet!

Planet named after the Roman God of the Sea

Dwarf Planets, Asteroids, Comets

As well as the Sun and the planets, there are lots of other bodies in our Solar System...

Dwarf Planets!

There are five recognised dwarf planets in our Solar System: Ceres, Pluto, Haumea, Makemake, and Eris, but scientists believe that there may be hundreds, or even thousands in all!

Can you find stickers of some things astronauts may need to take with them on space missions?

Spacesuit

Rocket

Lunar Buggy

Space Shuttle

Space Food

Asteroids!

Asteroids are big chunks of rock and metal – some are very large, and even have their own moons!

Most of the asteroids in our Solar System circle the sun in the Asteroid Belt.

Sometimes, an asteroid falls to the Earth, but this is very unusual. Some scientists believe that the dinosaurs were wiped out when an asteroid hit the Earth 65 million years ago!

Comets

Comets are made of rock, dust, snow, and ice.

As they travel closer to the Sun they begin to melt; this is what give's them their tail!

Meteoroids

Meteoroids are smaller chunks of rock and metal that have fallen off of asteroids and comets.

Sometimes, a meteoroid falls through the Earth's atmosphere, and becomes a meteor.

If the meteor falls all the way down to Earth it is called a meteorite.

Around 3,000 meteorites hit the Earth every year! Because most of the Earth's surface is covered in water, most of them fall into the sea.

Did you know...?

- It takes 13 hours to reach the moon in a rocket!

- It would take 139 days to drive to the moon in a car!

Wonders of Learning

Sticker Book